J 4
Bryar   W9-AUU-876
The many kinds of clean

$25.65
ocn829098102
04/01/2014

The Many Kinds of
Clean

by Dale-Marie Bryan

amicus readers

Ideas for Parents and Teachers

Amicus Readers let children practice reading informational texts at the earliest reading levels. Familiar words and concepts with close photo-text matches support early readers.

Before Reading

- Discuss the cover photo with the child. What does it tell him?
- Ask the child to predict what she will learn in the book.

Read the Book

- "Walk" through the book and look at the photos. Let the child ask questions.
- Read the book to the child, or have the child read independently.

After Reading

- Use the picture glossary at the end of the book to review the text.
- Prompt the child to make connections. Ask: What are other words for clean?

Amicus Readers are published by Amicus
P.O. Box 1329, Mankato, MN 56002
www.amicuspublishing.us

Library of Congress
Cataloging-in-Publication Data
Bryan, Dale-Marie, 1953-
 The many kinds of clean / Dale-Marie Bryan.
  pages cm. -- (So many synonyms)
 ISBN 978-1-60753-508-9 (hardcover) -- ISBN 978-1-60753-537-9 (eBook)
 1. English language--Synonyms and antonyms--Juvenile literature. I. Title.
 PE1591.B76 2013
 428.1--dc23
                    2013006844

Photo Credits: Shutterstock Images, cover, 4, 5, 9, 13, 14, 16 (top left), 16 (middle right), 16 (bottom left), 16 (bottom right); Africa Studio/Shutterstock Images, 1, 6, 7, 16 (middle left); Monkey Business Images/Shutterstock Images, 3; Good Mood Photo/Shutterstock Images, 10, 11, 16 (top right)

Produced for Amicus by The Peterson Publishing Company and Red Line Editorial.

Editor Jenna Gleisner
Designer Becky Daum
Printed in the United States of America
Mankato, MN
1-2014
PO1192
10 9 8 7 6 5 4 3 2

Kevin cleans his room. Do you know any words that mean clean? Words with similar meanings are synonyms.

3

Tidy means clean.

The bed is tidy when it is made. Kevin tucks in the sheets. He puts the pillows at the top.

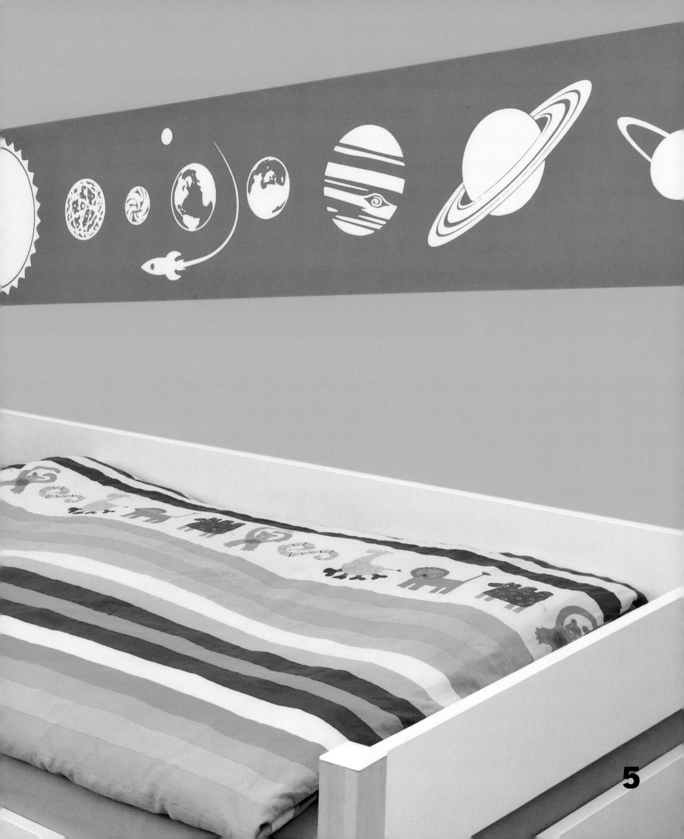

Neat means clean.

The desk is **neat** when messes are cleaned. Kevin wipes up spills. He puts pencils in holders.

Orderly means clean.

Kevin makes the shelf orderly.
He turns all of the books to
face the same way.

9

Spotless means clean.

Kevin hangs up **spotless** shirts after they are washed.

Spick and span means clean.

The bedroom is spick and span when everything is clean. Kevin sweeps the floor. He dusts the shelves.

14

Sparkling means clean.

The window is sparkling after it is wiped. Sunlight sparkles through the clean window in the morning. It is time for Kevin to start the day!

Synonyms for Clean

tidy
neat

spotless
without spots

neat
put away

spick and span
very clean

orderly
in order

sparkling
shiny

16